Christmas Programs for the Church

Number 13

Compiled by
Judith Ann Sparks

Cover by
Camerique

STANDARD PUBLISHING
Cincinnati, Ohio   2613

ISBN: 0-87239-392-5

© 1980. The STANDARD PUBLISHING COMPANY, Cincinnati, Ohio.
Division of STANDEX INTERNATIONAL CORPORATION.
Printed in U.S.A.

Contents

Monologue for Christmas

by Suzanne Holt

Here He is . . . I can't believe *I'm* here, too, just standing and looking at the Messiah.

We've waited for this time; we've hoped for this time—though I'm sure we'd all begun to wonder if we'd live to see it.

What a night! It was so terrifying when the angel appeared . . . as if the field was all "on fire." And then in his mighty booming voice he told us the news that today our Savior was born in Bethlehem—and we'd find Him right here in a manger.

So . . . *this* is the Son of God—this tiny baby . . . Somehow it's not what I expected . . .

But then, what *did* I expect? Perhaps a *little* more glory and majesty—I don't know . . .

Baby clothes of fancy, sparkly stuff—certainly of richer quality than these simple strips of material I see; a little golden rattle; a royal crib instead of this cowfeed box filled with straw; the emperor's suite in a classy inn rather than this dirty stable full of animals; a nursing staff of angels gleaming in white . . .

But there's just Mary here . . . and Joseph . . .
with Him.

It's probably pretty ridiculous, but I guess that's the picture I had in *my* mind.

Well, look . . . He's . . . crying . . .

Jesus, God's own Son, is crying—just like my own son cried . . . just like I cried when I was a baby.

What can that mean? I'm just not sure I understand. I mean, I *know* God is right here *with* us. That's what the prophet said; he said He'd be right here on the earth with us. But I didn't figure it to be like this. I just never thought—*He'd* cry. **But He** *is* . . . **crying** . . .

My . . . I guess God REALLY *is* "WITH US"—like I'm *with* my friends. He's going through what every one of us human beings has experienced—all those little irritations of being a baby . . . hunger . . . upset stomach . . . rashes. . . .

Amazing . . .

And He'll have to go through "teething" and learning to walk . . . even learning to talk—all those traumas and all those joys of growing up. God . . . RIGHT here . . . RIGHT beside us . . . *one* of us. He was willing to become one of us.

So when *we* cry, He'll understand. When we laugh, He'll understand. If we struggle, trip, or fall, He'll understand . . . because He's been here—WITH us.

It's hard to grasp . . .

God *WITH* us in the form of a little baby who eats, sleeps, gurgles . . . and cries—just like *I* did.

So—*THIS* is the "anointed one" that God promised and the prophets foretold . . . the one who will save us from the consequences of our failures and will lead us in the RIGHT ways . . .
Here in this very manger—

Lord God, I don't believe I understand how You're going to do it,
    but I believe You can and will.

I believe that somehow You—
    somehow this little baby—
    are going to make *ALL* the difference in the world.

6

What Christmas Is All About

by Ruth Blakeslee

(This Christmas program can be adapted for use by a small number of children, or it can use any number. The children like it because they are usually carrying something on stage, they appear several times, and the verses are short.)

Needed: A director
Pianist
Reader
Two or more older children or youth as helpers
Adults to dress the children in the manger scene
All the children

Props (in the order they are needed):
A copy of the script for the reader and one for each adult and youth helper
Something on which to attach the Christmas cards with tape or tacks (a folding screen works fine)
As many Christmas cards as you have children who will participate, preferably bright and colorful cards, showing a variety of subjects (do not use new cards)
Wreath
Candle
Bells

Lightweight artificial Christmas tree (decorated with unbreakable ornaments)
Pretty wrapped gifts
Cans of food
Book of Christmas carols
Star with heavy, double-coated tape on the back
Bible
Manger, two low stools
Doll in a white blanket
Wings for the angels (made of white nylon net with wire inserted to frame them, have ties to come around and tie in front, and pins to anchor them in the back)
Shepherds crooks, three or more (use tree limbs or get a man handy in his workshop to make them)
Containers for the Wise-men (wooden, brass, or painted gold)
Three crowns for the Wise-men (cardboard decorated as you like)
White robes for angels (possibly baptismal gowns)
Gold or silver band for angel's head (possibly tree garland)
Bathrobes for Joseph, the shepherds, and Wise-men
Long dress and head scarf for Mary

(Begin with screen to hold cards in center stage. Have the reader to one side. Children are ready to come in, each holding a Christmas card.)

Reader: Ah, Chistmas is here again! I love Christmas, but I understand that sometimes adults forget what Christmas really means. They get tired. Christmas, with all its rush, and bustle, and planning, is almost too much. What they want to do is to go to sleep December 1 and take a long nap, not waking till Christmas is all over! I think we need to be reminded that Christmas is a wonderful time. The children are going to do just that; they're going to tell us once more what Christmas is all about.

(Pianist plays a lively Christmas tune while the children

enter and stand at their sitting area.)

Reader: Christmas begins early in December, when the mailman starts to leave cheerful greetings in the mailbox. The children want to share their greetings with you.

(All the children display their cards, tell what is on them [one at a time], place them on the screen, then go to seating area and remain standing. One or two older youth are needed to hold the screen to keep it from falling.)

Examples: My card says "Hi"
Mine says "Season's Greetings"
Mine says "Happy Caroling"
My card shows the snow
Mine has a fat Santa
Mine has the manger scene
Mine has the shepherds
Mine has the Wise-men

In unison: They all say "Merry Christmas!"

(Now the children may be seated.)

Reader: And then, to stir us up and get us in the right mood for Christmas, we start to decorate our homes. We put a wreath on the door.

Child: The wreath on the door
Is more than just show;
It's sending our love
To everyone we know.

Reader: We place candles here and there.

Child: If we show we love other people,
By the acts of kindness we do,
Then we're obeying what Jesus told us,
And our lives are like candles, too.

Reader: Sometimes we decorate with bells.

Child: Bells are to keep us happy—
       In a joyful mood.
       We mustn't frown at Christmas,
       But go about doing good.

Reader: And then we find a Christmas tree—and place it near a window for all to adore.

(Youth bring in a decorated tree and place it to one side on the stage.)

Child: A Christmas tree is always green,
       It never dies away—
       And that's what Jesus means to me:
       His love is here to stay!

Reader: It's *fun* to decorate the Christmas tree! Why do grown-ups think it's work?

Child: It's fun to decorate the tree,
       With every pretty thing I may—
       And then it's fun to see it sparkle,
       Each time I glance its way!

Reader: Then, under the Christmas tree, we place gifts—for the people we love. The gifts tonight are for our nursing home friends (or to others; your choice). We give because:

Child: That first Christmas God gave us
       The most wonderful gift of all—
       His only Son, baby Jesus,
       Born in a Bethlehem stall.

(Children place their gifts.)

Reader: Tonight the children also have gifts for the needy in our community, because Christmas is always a time for sharing.

Child: "Love," Jesus said,

"In both feeling and deed."
"Share," Jesus said,
"With your brother in need."

(Children place cans of food in a basket or box.)

Reader: What would December be without the Christmas carols?

Child: I love the Christmas carols—
    To hear them and to sing
    About the joys of Christmas—
    And the babe who's now our king!

(Children come on center stage and sing "Away in a Manger." Use as many other carols as you like.)

Reader: Christmas is a special star.

Child: Christmas is a special star
    To mark that wondrous birth.
    The birth that was God's gift to man—
    Living all over the earth.

(Child gives star to youth, who places it high on the wall.)

Reader: Christmas is a time to go to the Bible.

Child: Christmas we go to the Bible,
    God's Holy Word,
    To read the story of Jesus
    That first the shepherds heard.

(Child places the manger for scene; another child, or a youth, places a low stool on either side of the manger.)

Reader: Christmas is Joseph and Mary.

Child: Christmas is Joseph—
    A carpenter far from home.

Child: And Mary, sweet young woman,

11

God chose for His plan divine.

(Joseph and Mary sit either side of the manger, on low stools.)

Reader: But, mostly, Christmas is a baby.

Child: Christmas is a baby,
Come down to earthly sod,
Whose mother is sweet Mary—
Whose Father is our God.

(Child places wrapped doll in the manger and takes a position behind Mary.)

Reader: Christmas is the angels.

Child: Christmas is the angels
Come down from Heaven above,
To spread the news, in music sweet,
Of the birth of the King of love.

(Angel takes a place behind Joseph.)

Reader: Christmas is the lowly shepherds.

(If there is a shortage of children, the reader may read the poems for the remainder of the program.)

Child: Christmas is the lowly shepherds,
Who left their flocks and their fires,
To find the babe the angels told them
Held the world's promise and desires.

(Shepherds come slowly up center aisle, carrying crooks. They kneel before the manger.)

Reader: Christmas is the Wise-men.

Child: Christmas is the Wise-men,
Who traveled far and near,

Because the new star told them
The Savior of the world was here!

(Wise-men come slowly up center aisle, carrying containers. They kneel.)

Reader: And, lastly, Christmas is a prayer.

Older youth: Let us pray.
Dear Father, who art in Heaven,
How splendid was that night!
You shunned the glamour of the world;
You shunned the castles bright;
You chose a humble maiden,
A stable behind an inn,
And shepherds close to nature
When the Savior's life began.
Help us to crowd out the glamour, Lord,
The world's heavy noise and bright sights,
And to appreciate all the wonder
Of your holiest of holy nights! Amen.

Reader: Ah, friends, please don't hate Christmas.
Don't close your hearts and wish it gone!
'Tis the most wonderful time of all the year—
Let's celebrate in song!

(All sing "Joy to the World!")

The Night the Child Was Born

by Rega Kramer McCarty

(Off center to the left of the stage [slightly back] a manger scene is set. An unlighted star [to be lit later] hangs overhead. As the scene opens, no one except readers are on stage. Readers stand on each side of the manger, perhaps slightly toward front. To right of stage have a stool placed for Mary to sit on when the Wise-men come.)

Rebekah: Early in the evening
Of this marvelous day,
I, Rebekah, maid of the inn,
Heard the keeper say,
"There is no room—
No room in all of Bethlehem."
He looked upon the weary pair
With compassion in his eyes for them.

The lovely woman waited—
Great with child was she—
She listened as the stalwart man
Made an earnest plea.
The keeper saw that they had come
As far as she was able,
So he offered them a bed of hay,
Within the fresh-cleaned stable.

(Stable scene lights up with soft lights, yet lights bright enough for each detail to be seen by audience.)

Jonas: I, Jonas, stable boy, was present
When the man and woman came.
I heard him call her Mary—
How tenderly he said her name!
She called him Joseph as she settled on the hay,
And, before I left them there,
I saw him kneel and bow his head
As they spoke in quiet prayer.

(The above scene is done in pantomime as Jonas speaks. As they are in attitudes of prayer, lights go out.)

I was restless through the night—
Many strangers were in the town—
They had come to pay their taxes,
For Herod's edict had come down.
Then through my windowpane I saw
Lights of brilliant sheen (star lights up)—
High in the heavens!
Were the brightest stars I'd ever seen!
Quickly reaching for my tunic
I hurried out the door.
Outside there were voices and awailing
I had never heard before.
Then Rebekah stood beside me,
And we went to see what it could be!

(Readers may remain in their places or could, if desired, approach the manger scene.)

Rebekah: We found Mary with a baby at her breast—
A look of holy joy upon her face—
These three were surely blessed!
Then we heard footsteps fast approaching,
As shepherds came from the hills,
"We have come to find the Savior,
To pay Him homage as God wills."

(Shepherds enter and kneel to worship the child.)

Jonas: While the shepherds knelt in wonder,
Joseph watched the reverent scene—
His eyes alert for danger,
But all was quiet and serene.

(Dim lights and while music is played, have Mary move to stool on right side of stage. She holds baby in her arms while Joseph stands near.)

Some time later a man of marked distinction—
With a gift in hand—
Approached Joseph and said, "We have come
To see the King of man."

(The Wise-men in Biblical dress enact scene above. Joseph indicates baby in Mary's arms.)

Rebekah: When Joseph pointed toward the child,
They seemed to be amazed,
But they moved inside the room
And knelt in reverent praise.
These, the Wise-men from the East,
Had traveled long and far;
They came with frankincense, gold, and myrrh,
Following God's symbol, the star.

(Wise-men lay gifts near the baby and kneel to worship also.)

Jonas: And as they kneel to worship Him—
Lord of lords and King of kings—
Angel voices proclaim in song
The joy and hope His coming brings!

(Chorus offstage sings an appropriate song—first in low voices, then louder as speakers cease their readings.)

A bright new day has dawned at last
For the men of faith throughout the earth.
God has fulfilled His promised Word,
With the Christ child's holy birth!

Program for a Small Group

Bethlehem—Christmas for All the World

by Edith Beach Sipple

Background music: "O Little Town of Bethlehem"

On stage: Manger, Mary, and Joseph
       Two girls dressed in white pull the curtains.

Opening: Girls' trio sings first stanza of "O Little Town of Bethlehem."

Boy enters: Reads from a scroll he carries.

"He demanded of them where Christ should be born. And they said unto him, In Bethlehem of Judea: for thus it is written by the prophet, And thou Bethlehem, in the land of Judah, art not the least among the princes of Judah: for out of thee shall come a Governor, that shall rule my people Israel."

Song: Choir sings second stanza of "O Little Town of Bethlehem."

Reader (dressed in white): Stands to one side and reads loudly.

Bethlehem a city of Judah,
Bethlehem the birthplace of David,
Bethlehem the birthplace of Jesus of Nazareth, the Son of God,

17

Brought Christmas to all lands everywhere,
Brought Christmas to all peoples everywhere,
Brought Christmas to all the world.
Bethlehem!

(Different children enter. Have ribbons with the name of the country they represent pinned to one shoulder and draped down across the front of their bodies.)

Asia enters:

Asia, civilizations of the past—
Perhaps the first on earth.
From our continent Abraham was sent.
A new nation would come to be,
God promised as he went
To Israel the promised land
Where Christ was born in Bethlehem.

Israel enters:

Israel's known throughout the world
As the birthplace of the King of kings.
Prophesied by prophets bold,
We kneel where Christ was born we're told.
Oh, yes, say it again and again,
Jesus the Lord was born in Bethlehem.

Song: Choir sings third stanza of "O Little Town of Bethlehem."

England enters:

In merry ole England carolers sing,
While in the distance church bells ring.
In each home the yule log burns for you and me,
Where we're invited in for tea.
England believes that Jesus came for them
Nearly two thousand years ago in Bethlehem.

Germany enters:

In Germany we use evergreen trees
That point to the sky from whence Jesus came.
No other tree ever grew quite the same.
We put the candles and lights on it—

18

To look like stars bright.
For we believe that Jesus was born in Bethlehem
One starry night!

U.S.A. enters:

Christmas is lots of fun in the U.S.A.,
For here hearts are light and gay.
Gifts galore are given,
But no gift was ever so precious,
And none can give more,
Than God gave
That night in Bethlehem!

All kneel around the manger: Softly sing last stanza of "O
Little Town of Bethlehem."

19

Kevin and His Trumpet

by Aileen Mallory

Characters: Mrs. Carlton, older girl
Mr. Carlton, older boy
Judy, 8 to 10
Mark, 6 to 8
Debbie, 10 to 12
Cheryl, 10 to 12
Kevin, 10 to 12
Carolers (regular choir may also be offstage)
Trumpeter (may be adult; offstage)

Setting: Carlton living room. Usual furniture, with clock on wall or table. One entrance is at right, the other either left or center back.

Scene I

(Scene opens to show Mrs. Carlton and Mark. She is seated, sewing or reading, and he is playing on the floor. Noise of children outside. Mark runs to door, right.)

Mark: Here they are, Mama.

Mrs. Carlton (rising): Good. I was wondering why they were so late.

20

(ENTER Judy, Debbie, and Carol, from right.)

Debbie: Sorry we're late, Mom. We stayed to practice Christmas carols.

Cheryl (starts back toward door, right): I have to get on home or Mother will be worrying about me.

Debbie: Wait a minute, Cheryl. Stay while we talk over our problem with Mother. Maybe she will have some ideas.

Mrs. Carlton: Problem? What problem?

Judy: Kevin Lane. *He's* our problem.

Mrs. Carlton: Kevin? Why? He seems like a very nice boy to me.

Debbie: He's going to spoil our caroling. It will be a *disaster!* (Other children nod their heads, frowning.)

Mrs. Carlton: Why will he spoil it? I should think the more children who sing, the better it will sound.

Judy: Not with Kevin.

Debbie: Mother, you've never heard him. He sounds just terrible. He always sings way off-key.

Cheryl: What's more, he sings *loud*.

Mrs. Carlton (smiling): Well, I can sympathize with Kevin. I cannot carry a tune, either. The only time I sing— which is always off-key—is when the vacuum cleaner is running. (All laugh.)

Debbie: Do you remember the time Daddy played that trick on you?

Mrs. Carlton: Indeed I do!

Debbie (to others): One time, when Mother was vacuum-
  ing, Daddy had me slip outdoors and then knock on the
  front door like I was a neighbor or somebody. Daddy
  went to the door and said in a loud voice, "No, lady,
  I'm not beating my wife. She is singing." (All laugh.)

Mark: Daddy wouldn't beat up on Mama.

Judy: Of course not, Mark. It was just a joke. (To her
  mother.) But *you* aren't going caroling, Mother. What
  will we do about Kevin?

Cheryl: Maybe he will decide not to go.

Debbie: Are you kidding? He is so enthusiastic about it that
  he wouldn't miss it for the world. His folks moved here
  after Christmas last year, so he's never had a chance to
  go caroling before.

Mrs. Carlton: And you just cannot ask him to stay home.

All: No, no. (Shake their heads.)

Mrs. Carlton: No, of course not.

Debbie: Mom, we can't hurt his feelings. You know that.
  (All sit quietly, thinking.)

Mrs. Carlton: What does your Sunday-school teacher say
  about it? Have you talked it over with her? After all,
  she is the one who is in charge of your caroling.

Judy (rather disgusted): Oh, we talked to her all right. Miss
  Phillips says we are just to pretend that Kevin is in tune
  and sing along like everything is okay. But that's pretty
  hard to do when he sings so awful, and so *loud*.

Debbie: That's because he enjoys it so much. (All pretend
  to groan, etc.)

(Knock at door, right.)

Mark: I'll go, I'll go. (Goes to door. Enter Kevin, carrying trumpet.)

Judy: Well! Hi, Kevin. How are you?

Kevin: Oh, I'm okay. Just like I was when you saw me a little while ago. (All laugh.) My won't caroling be fun? I can hardly wait!

Mrs. Carlton: How's your mother, Kevin? We missed her at _____ yesterday. (Use name of local church women's group.)

Kevin: Oh, she's okay now. She had a bad headache yesterday, she said. Daddy sent me over here now to see if Mr. Carlton has a wrench he can borrow. Dad said he was going to phone.

Mrs. Carlton: He hasn't called yet, Kevin, and Mr. Carlton isn't home from the office. But he should be here any minute so you can ask him. I'm sure it will be all right.

Mark (staring at Kevin's trumpet): Where did you get that horn, Kevin?

Judy: That's a trumpet, Mark. You carry it with you just about everywhere you go, don't you, Kevin?

Kevin (smiling): Yes, I guess I do. I'm sorta crazy about this trumpet. (Looks at it fondly.)

Cheryl: Not only crazy about it, but good at it. Mrs. Carlton, you should hear him play that trumpet!

Debbie: He really is good. I wish I could play my clarinet half as well.

Kevin: Oh, well, I practice a lot.

Cheryl (looking at clock): I'd better get home! If Mother calls, tell her I'm on my way. (Debbie sees Cheryl to the door, right.)

Mrs. Carlton: It's getting dark outside. Judy, why don't you run down to Daddy's workshop and get his wrench for Kevin? I know he won't care, and Kevin probably wants to get on home. (Judy exits, left.)

Kevin: Gee, thanks. Tell Mr. Carlton we'll bring it back tomorrow.

Mark: I'm getting hungry.

Mrs. Carlton: Yes, I know you probably are. I guess we'll go ahead and eat, and Daddy can eat when he gets here.

(Judy returns; gives wrench to Kevin.)

Kevin: Thanks again. I'll be seein' you. (Exits, right.)

Debbie (eagerly): I think I just had a brainstorm, and I could hardly wait until Kevin left to tell you! I know what we can do about him and our caroling!!!

Judy: What? What? (All look at Debbie, questioningly.)

Debbie: Remember how our minister has the Jensen twins blow their trumpets before special services? Well . . . We were talking about how good Kevin is on his trumpet, so . . .

Judy: Of course! Kevin can be a trumpeter caroler.

Debbie: I can hardly wait for us to ask Miss Phillips if it is okay, and I bet she'll agree. I think all the others will, too. I'm going to call Cheryl and tell her!

Mrs. Carlton: Don't you think you should at least give her time to get home? You girls—you can see each other one minute and get on the telephone the next! (All laugh.) Now, let's go eat. (All exit.)

Scene II

(Same setting. Scene opens to show Mr. and Mrs. Carlton and Mark in living room.)

Mark: I wish I could go caroling.

Mrs. Carlton: Next year, Mark. Then your class will be included with the others.

Mr. Carlton: How about giving your recitation for the Christmas program, Son? Do you realize that I haven't even heard it yet?

Mark: Boy, you should have been around here. I've been practicing it over and over.

Mrs. Carlton: Indeed he has. I'm sure we both know every word. (Laughs.) (Noise at right.)

Mark: They're here, they're here! I'll speak my piece some other time, Dad.

Mrs. Carlton: I'll put some hot chocolate on the stove.

(Exits, left. Mr. Carlton and Mark go to door, right. Trumpet offstage plays "Hark! the Herald Angels Sing" or any favorite carol, followed by carolers and/or choir. Mrs. Carlton returns and stands by Mr. Carlton and Mark.)

Mr. Carlton: Come on in, and warm yourselves!

Mrs. Carlton: Why, that was just beautiful. The trumpet adds so much to the music. (If time permits, other carols may be sung, all with trumpet leading off.)

Mrs. Carlton: Do come in, and have some hot chocolate. (Carolers start coming in, Judy in the lead.)

25

Judy: Wasn't Kevin great, Mom? Everybody says that our caroling is better this year than it has ever been!

Mrs. Carlton: Yes, indeed. I guess everybody has something that he or she can give at Christmas, but it isn't always the same thing. We all can praise God and the Christ child in our own way.

Mr. Carlton (puts his arm around her): That's right, Dear. Come on everybody. (All enter, laughing and talking. Mrs. Carlton goes out, left, and comes back in with tray holding a pitcher and cookies. Mr Carlton helps her, as carolers gather around for their hot chocolate and cookies.)

Curtain

A One-Act Play With Five Scenes

Jesus, God and Man

by Jerry Millard Davidson

Characters: Narrator
Angel
Mary
Joseph
Shepherds (2 or 3)
Jesus (as a boy of 12)
Wise men in temple (3 or 4)
Jesus (as a man)
Disciples (3)

Scene 1

(Curtain is closed. Narrator stands at left in front of curtain.)

Narrator: "In the beginning was the Word, and the Word was with God, and the Word was God." Part of the Trinity came to earth, not just to visit as the angels have done, but to live here for a time. John 1:14 relates it this way: "And the Word was made flesh, and dwelt among us. . . . full of grace and truth." The four gospels of Matthew, Mark, Luke, and John record the story of God among men. Christians have always

27

found the mysterious mingling of mortal flesh and Divine Spirit both fascinating and beautiful. There are many places in the Bible where it is evident. We are going to show you some of them tonight.

(Enter Angel and stands at right of curtain.)

Angel: When I told the virgin Mary that she was to have a son who would be the Savior of the world, Mary at first thought only of the physical side. "I have never known a man," she said. "How can I have a child?"

I explained that the child would be the Son of God, fathered by the Holy Spirit. This answered her question, but she still seemed puzzled. What a remarkable handmaiden of the Lord she truly was to take my statement on faith!

To Mary was born this child that was prophesied.

(Curtain opens to reveal manger scene, Mary, Joseph, and the babe.)

Angel: It was a man-child that Mary wrapped in swaddling clothes and laid in the manger, because there was no room for them in the inn. He had the same sweet flesh, soft and innocent, that every mother knows. But, later on that night, it was Jesus, the Son of God, that the shepherds came to see.

(Enter the shepherds and kneel in front of the manger.)

Song: "The First Noel"

(Curtain closes between first and second verses to give time to change scene.)

Scene 2

Narrator: When this babe grew to be a young boy of twelve, He traveled to Jerusalem for the Passover as was the custom of His family. This time, though, something unusual happened. Jesus stayed behind without asking permission from His folks or even informing them.

(Curtain opens to show Jesus, as boy, seated on floor in front of three or four wise men in the temple. He gestures and talks, silently, while they listen attentively.)

Narrator: It was the boy, the son of Joseph and Mary, who stayed behind. It was Jesus, the Son of God, that the worried parents found in the temple talking to the learned men.

(Enter Joseph and Mary. Jesus rises to meet them.)

Jesus told them as much when He answered their question. "Know ye not that I must be about my Father's business?"

(Jesus, Joseph, and Mary exit.)

Still, the lad went home obediently with them, and we hear no more of Him until He reaches manhood.

(Curtain closes.)

Scene 3

Narrator: When John the Baptist began his preaching, Jesus came to him to be baptized. It was Jesus, the man, who was immersed in the waters of the Jordan River. It was the Divine One that the voice of God spoke to from Heaven saying, "Thou art my beloved Son; in thee I am well pleased."

When the multitude gathered to hear Jesus speak stayed long enough to be hungry, and there was only five loaves and two fishes to feed them all, it was Jesus, the man, who told His friends, "Bring them hither to me." But it was Jesus, the Bread of Life, who touched the food and multiplied it into enough to feed the five thousand.

(Curtain opens to show a boat against a backdrop of stormy skies. Jesus is asleep at one end of the boat. The disciples awaken Him during the narrator's speech, and He arises and stands with hands outstretched over the stormy waves. A real boat, or one of painted cardboard boxes, can be used with crepe paper waves.)

Narrator: It is recorded in Luke 8:23 that Jesus fell asleep in the ship when He and His disciples were crossing the Sea of Galilee. When a storm came up suddenly, it was Jesus, the weary man, that His friends awakened, crying, "We perish, Master! Awake!" But the one who said, "Peace, be still," and the waters and winds obeyed, was the One who had spoken in the beginning of the world. "Let there be a firmament in the midst of the waters, and let it divide the waters from the waters." No wonder the winds and the waves obeyed!

(Curtain closes.)

Song: "Master, the Tempest Is Raging"

Scene 4

Narrator: When the time for His death had almost come, was it Jesus the man or the mighty Son of God who sought a place alone to pray, seeking what He needed for the ordeal ahead? We don't know which one. Still, it was the simple carpenter from Nazareth who woke His three companions and told them, "Let us go. The hour is come when the Son of man is betrayed."

It was the tanned cheek of a man who spent His hours outdoors that Judas kissed in betrayal. It was the Great Healer who touched the head of a Roman soldier and replaced the ear cut off by the overzealous friend of Jesus during the arrest.

(Curtain opens. The stage is dark. On a dark background the shape of a large cross is outlined. The cross can be painted white and outlined with flourescent tape so it will glow in the dark.)

Narrator: The end came at last. After the mockery of a trial, the soldiers nailed a condemned man to the cross. Only a man like the other two beside him, who also bled from the nails in their hands and feet. It was only a mortal throat that thirsted, but the voice that told the repentant thief, "Today shalt thou be with me in paradise," was the kind and powerful Son of God.

Song: "Were You There When They Crucified My Lord?"

Angel: The dead flesh of the Word that came to earth to dwell among men was placed in the tomb. What a tragic ending if the narrative stopped there; if there were no more to tell. Thank God it is not all! The mysterious, invisible force that is Jesus, the Son of God, could apply that power to himself. So, Jesus, the man, and Christ, the Son of God, lives again, and we can celebrate His glorious resurrection.

(Gradually highlight the cross with a spotlight during the angel's speech.)

Angel: He left to all who believe on Him, as a man who was also the Son of God, the gift of eternal life, that is the Christmas gift God gave to the world.

(Curtain closes.)

Song: "Christ Arose!"

Scene 5

(Curtain opens to show manger scene again.)

Narrator: There has never been a chronicle in the history of mankind that is as endearing or earthshaking as the one the angel began in Luke 2:10.

Angel: "Fear not: for, behold, I bring you good tidings of great joy, which shall be to all people. For unto you is born this day in the city of David a Saviour, which is Christ the Lord."

Narrator: Man and God together. It had never happened before. It was never to happen again. This is the Christmas story, and it is a joy to bring it to you tonight.

Song: "O Holy Night" (solo) or "Silent Night, Holy Night" (Chorus)

(Curtain closes.)

Coos Bay 1980

Happy Birthday, Dear Jesus

by Jane K. Priewe

(This service is centered around button pins [bought or made as a Sunday-school project] carrying the message, HAPPY BIRTHDAY, DEAR JESUS! All Sunday-school children will wear a button, and there should be enough extras so that adults can be given one as they enter the church for the Christmas service. Older children can be stationed at doors to hand out the buttons.)

Button instructions: Make buttons from stiff, white poster paper. Print *HAPPY BIRTHDAY, DEAR JESUS* on the white circle in red. Draw a cross and simple manger in green. (Use other colors, if you prefer.) Punch two holes near the button's top and thread green or red ribbon through. Tie the ribbon to a small or medium sized safety pin, which has been sprayed with green or red paint.

Button costume: Cut out two large circles from a cardboard carton. Make these large enough to cover from a child's shoulders to his knees. Paint these two circles to look like the birthday buttons. Turn them into shoulder signs by attaching them together with wide pieces of white cloth. The child's head goes through opening between pieces of cloth, which rest across carrier's shoulders. (Make enough button costumes for the buttons in the play.)

Button banner: Make the banner from felt that is the same colors as the buttons and button costumes. Be sure it's big enough to be seen clearly from any seat in your hall or church.

Happy Birthday, Dear Jesus By Jane K. Priewe

X **Processional:** "O Come, All Ye Faithful" (Led by a banner carrier and four children in button costumes. The banner is posted where all can see it and the children exit.)

Beginners Sing Happy Birthday, Jesus

Reader 1 (offstage or onstage voice; your choice): This is not only a Christmas service, it is a birthday celebration—the most important birthday the world has ever known. The night baby Jesus was born was different. Stars twinkled and winked in a velvety sky. One bright star out-sparkled all the others. It seemed to say, "This is a special night! Come and see! Spread the news!"

Song: "O Little Town of Bethlehem" (For special effect, at the end of each verse or just at the end of the hymn, have a small group of children's voices sing a soft benediction: "Happy Birthday, Dear Jesus.")

Reader 2: Luke 2:4-7 (This could be a solo or a choral recitation.)

Reader 3: Even though there was no birthday party with games, or cake, or ice cream, or candles for the baby in the manger, some guests *did* come to see Him. These guests weren't kings, or queens, or rich, or famous people. They were humble shepherds who were tending their flocks in a field not too far from the stable. An angel appeared, telling them the Savior had been born, and a heavenly chorus sang praises to God. After the angels had returned to Heaven, the shepherds hurried away to see the Christ child. They were excited because, at last, God's promise of a long-awaited Savior had been fulfilled.

34

Song: "Away in a Manger" (Special effect same as previous hymn.)

Reader 4: Luke 2:18 (Again this could be onstage or offstage voice; solo or chorale recitation.)

Reader 5: The shepherds weren't the only visitors to come to see Jesus. Faraway in the East, Wise-men saw a sign that told them the Savior was born. They followed the star to Jerusalem and asked: "Where is he that is born King of the Jews? for we have seen his star in the east, and are come to worship him." They brought gifts of gold and frankincense and myrrh, which they gave to Mary and Joseph for the baby Jesus.

Song: "We Three Kings of Orient Are" (Use same special effect.)

Reader 6: Matthew 2:9-11 (Solo or chorale recitation on or off the stage.)

Collection: (Hymn of your choice for congregation to sing together.)

Busy Birthday Buttons

Beginners: sing Happy Birthday Jesus

(Children in button costumes take places on stage.)

Reader 7: Everyone of us will wear a "Happy Birthday" button home this evening. Hopefully, you will continue to wear it where it can easily be seen and read by anyone you meet during this Christmas season. If you should get one of our talking buttons, what kind of an owner will you be?

Button 1: I don't want to leave our cozy button box. I'm afraid to go home with a stranger.

Button 2: You knew when we were painted and stamped that we were to spread the message. You're a chicken!

Button 3: He is? I thought we were buttons!

35

Button 4: Of course, we're buttons! And we *have* to leave our button box.

Button 1: (Wails, wrings hands, and pretends to cry.) I'm not *ready* to leave! Oh, dear! Oh, dear!

Button 5: Now, what's wrong? You're acting just terrible on Jesus' birthday!

Button 1: (Hangs head, scuffs foot.) I've forgotten the message.

Button 6: (Acts surprised.) So have *I*! What *is* the message?

Button 7: I can't *believe* this! It's almost time for us to leave our button box, and you two don't know the message! It's, *"Go and tell!"*

Button 1: Oh, sure! Now, I remember!

Button 6: So do I.

Button 8: I should hope you do! We're to go and tell that Jesus was born so He could die on the cross for us. (Shouts.) Worship and work, Buttons!

Button 1: I thought you said the message was "Go and tell." Now you're yelling worship and work! You're getting me all mixed up!

Button 9: Me, too! Make up your mind! Which is the right message?

Button 10: (Sighs with frustration.) They're *both* right. If you go and tell, you'll worship and work for God.

Button 11: (Showing patience.) And if you worship and work, you'll just naturally go and tell. The shepherds did it, so we must do it, too.

Button 12: (Jiggles impatiently.) I want to get going! Who shall I tell, since we buttons already know?

Button 4: (Points to audience.) You tell whoever wears you. Personally, I hope *I* go home with a nonbeliever!

Button 1: What's a nonbeliever?

Button 2: Someone who doesn't believe in God or Jesus.

Button 3: (Nudges Button 1, shaking head.) Now, if that isn't stupid, I don't know what is! Why would any self-respecting button want to go home with someone like *that?*

Button 4: (Patiently explains.) Because it will be a challenge to get that person to think about Jesus, and how He died for our sins. Yes, I really *do* hope I get pinned to a nonbeliever's dress or jacket.

Button 5: Not me! I want to be worn by a little child, who's just started to come to Sunday school.

Button 6: That *does* sound nice! Even an older child might give us a good home. (Shakes Button 5's hand.) Congratulations for such a great idea! I'm proud of you!

Button 7: Forget about the good home bit. That's not important. Delivering the *message* is the main thing!

Button 8: That's right. How're you planning to give them the message, if little kids can't read?

Button 7: I know they can't read, but those in Sunday school believe in Jesus. They tell others about Him. Jesus even said, "Unless you change and become like little children, you will never enter the kingdom of heaven" (Matthew 18:3).

Button 9: A very good point! I think I'd prefer the child to a nonbeliever. I only hope I'll be worn by someone, large or small, who shares Jesus with others.

Button 10: (Acts excited.) At this time of year, almost everyone has a manger scene with the baby Jesus in it. What we have to do is take Jesus out of the manger and share Him with people.

Button 11: What a fine idea! I like it! (Shouts excitedly.) "Go and tell!"

Button 12: Like pastors and teachers spread the Word!

(Buttons nod and smile at each other.)

Button 1: Like elders and missionaries!

Button 2: Yes, even like choir singers. After all, they're spreading God's Word through music, aren't they?

(Buttons nod and do a little jig.)

Button 3: All these ideas are good, but if *I* don't get the kind of person *I* want, I'm going to break my pin and not go home with anyone!

(Buttons gasp, look shocked, shake heads, and move apart from 3.)

Button 4: What a *terrible* thing to say!

Button 5: For *shame* on you! (Points finger.)

Button 6: What kind of person do you *want?*

Button 3: (Struts back and forth.) I want a lazy Christian!

Button 7: A *lazy* Christian!

Button 8: What's that?

Button 9: It's one with sleeping sickness.

Button 3: (Snickers.) No, it isn't. A lazy Christian is a person who believes in Jesus, but doesn't care if anyone else does. It's a person who wouldn't sing in a choir even if he had a good voice.

Button 10: I know *that* type. They make a big show of liking children, and are smart enough to be teachers, but they won't help with Sunday school.

Button 11: Don't forget that lazy Christians can be children as well as grown-ups. Everybody could bring friends to church and Sunday school, but most times they can't be bothered. You know . . . (he droops) too lazy!

(Buttons nod and scowl.)

Button 12: What about the ones who put only a small love gift in the collection when they could share much more? They're lazy *and selfish!*

(Buttons nod and grumble.)

Button 3: Now you know why I want to go home with a lazy Christian. I'm going to sparkle, and look so interesting that people will ask what "Happy Birthday, Dear Jesus" means.

Button 4: (Throws arm over 3's shoulder.) And *your* lazy Christian will really have to think hard to come up with the right answer!

(Buttons laugh and clap.)

Button 1: No matter who wears us home, we'd do well to sparkle and look interesting. Shape up, Buttons! We're about to spread the message! Let's "Go and tell!"

Buttons together: Happy Birthday, Dear Jesus!
Happy Birthday, Christ child!
Happy Birthday, little King!
Happy Birthday, Son of God!
Merry Christmas to everyone! (Buttons exit.)

Congregation: (Sing to tune of "Hark! the Herald Angels Sing.")
"Happy Birthday, little Baby.
Birthday blessings, little King.
You have come to save all people,

39

Everlasting life You bring.
Joyful now we celebrate,
This year's most important date.
As we pray this holy night,
May our faith stay ever bright.
"Happy Birthday," we all sing.
"Happy Birthday," newborn King.

"Happy Birthday," God's own Son.
Birthday blessings, Holy One.
Sing we all, and raise our voice,
While the angel host rejoice.
Let us hear the wondrous story,
Of the Christ child's radiant glory.
How He came to save mankind.
Keep this ever in your mind.
"Happy Birthday," infant mild.
"Happy Birthday," God's own child.

Reader

Benediction: (Minister or someone you choose.)
(Lower lights and all sing, "Silent Night, Holy Night." At
end of hymn, echo "Happy Birthday, Dear Jesus.")

Recessional: "Joy to the World" (Led by banner carrier and
buttons.)

The Characters of Christmas

by Vickie R. Kilmer

Costumes: The traditional type of costumes may be used, but to make it different why not use poster costumes? Sketch or paste pictures on poster board and let the characters hold them in front of them. The pictures could be taken from old Bible-school literature or visuals packs.

Welcome
Four-year-olds can steal your heart,
And that's what I'm here to do.
I have a very important part,
I'm here to *WELCOME* you.

Twos and Threes
Jesus was once a boy like me.
So now like Him I want to be.

With a great big smile,
I'm here to say—
"Jesus, Happy Birthday."

Baby Jesus was His name,
I'm so very glad He came.

To Jesus—Happy Birthday.
To you—Happy Holiday.

I'm a big boy
Who wishes you joy
This Christmas.

A little girl
With pretty curls
Wants to say just this:
Merry Christmas.

Introduction

The characters of Christmas
We've come *tonight* to share,
To tell the Christmas story
To remind us of God's care.

or

The characters of Christmas
We've come to share *today,*
To tell the Christmas story
In our own special way.

We are glad you came to hear it.
Listen! Think about what is said.
We want to add more meaning
To the days that are just ahead.

Shepherd

Just watching our sheep in the field,
Nothing special, an ordinary night.
But from out of that lonely darkness,
There came a glorious light.

Shepherd

There appeared unto us angels—
A choir of heavenly beings.
Singing about a Savior
Who came to be our king.

Angel

> I was only one of many
> Who came down to sing
> About our Redeemer, our Savior, our king.

Angel

> We sang of a babe wrapped
>   in swaddling clothes.
> Sent to this world
>   God's love to show.

Shepherd

> Afraid? You bet!
> But the message was one of joy—
> About a babe in a manger,
> A precious baby boy.

Angel

> Peace on earth,
> Good will toward men.
> You'll find the babe in Bethlehem.

City of Bethlehem

> I am the city of David,
> Full of people to be counted and taxed.
> You know it best as Bethlehem,
> Where shepherds came to worship Him.

Shepherd

> We found the babe in Bethlehem,
> Just as we were told.
> A Savior, a king, the promised one,
> Only a few hours old.

Shepherd

> Keep it to ourselves, you say.
> Not us! We left rejoicing
> To share with others this blessed event.
> We told it gladly wherever we went.

Innkeeper

It was late when they came.
I had no room in my place.
But they accepted the stable
With a smile on their face.
It wasn't the best, but it was cozy and warm,
A small, lowly place for the babe to be born.

Stable

A stable, a small friendly stable,
That's all I was meant to be.
A place for the animals of travelers
Who stayed in the inn next to me.

But how different this night
Would turn out to be.
For the King of all kings
Was born inside me.

Manger

A babe in a manger
    so tiny and small.
He came to this world
    to love one and all.

Mary

My Son was so small as He laid in the hay.
There were so many things I wanted to say.
To think I was blessed to have such a part,
But I kept all these things quite close to my heart.

Joseph

I couldn't quite understand all that had taken place.
But I at once loved the smile on the baby's small face.
He was a miracle! Sent from above!
He was a miracle! A bundle of love!

Animals in the Stable

We had to scoot over to make room for the crowd,
Who came to see Jesus.
You know we were proud.

Star

    A star in the East
    Was what guided the men
    On their way to Bethlehem.

Wise-men

    We traveled so far the
        Christ child to see.
    My frankincense was a gift—
        One of the three.

Wise-man

    My myrrh smelled so good.
    It was the best I could bring
    To lay at the feet of the newborn king.

Wise-man

    Gold was the gift
    From an old, wise stranger.
    Given to the babe
    Who was born in the manger.

Cross

    You may not have seen me,
    But I was there just the same.
    For this is the reason the small baby came.
    He would die on the cross
        for you and for me.
    That we can have life and
        from sin be set free.

Gift

    A small baby boy
    Born that first Christmas eve.
    To bring down a gift that
        we *all* can receive.

Gift

    He knows you!
    He loves you!
    And He wants you to find,
    The joy, peace, and love

of that first Christmastime.

Closing
       The characters of Christmas
       We've shared with you *tonight*.
       We want you to know
       It's been our delight.

             or

       The characters of Christmas
       We've shared with you *today*.
       Thank you for coming,
       And we would just like to say,

       May your Christmas be happy.
       May your Christmas be bright.
       As you celebrate the birth
         of our Savior that night.

The Christmas Family

by Mary E. Campbell

"The Christmas Family" is an inspirational expression that can be done with married couples and single individuals of just about any age, as long as they are able to express themselves. Only one rehearsal is necessary, and that is for placement. No verbal rehearsal is required. It takes away from the experience.

Charity
Humility
Respect
Inspiration
Sincerity
Tolerance
Mercy
Assurance
Strength

Setting: Depends on facilities and arrangement of auditorium.

Clothing: No special clothing needed. You will need large letters to spell the word Christmas.

Presentation: Each couple or individual is given a letter from the word Christmas. They are to tell about an experience that shows how the word has worked in

47

their life. Their experience can be a joyful or sad experience, but it should be one that inspires and gives enlightenment to those listening.

Outline: Each couple or individual enters one at a time, beginning with the letter C (charity). After they have told about their experience, the couple or individual quotes a Scripture of their choosing that best exemplifies the point they are making. Then the couple or individual concludes by saying to the audience, "Our Christmas gift to you is what God has so graciously given us—charity," or whatever word they represent. They keep their position until the word Christmas is completely spelled. After all participants have spoken, they all say in unison, "Silver and gold have we none; but such as we have give we thee" (Acts 3:6, paraphrased).

Time: Allow 5 minutes for each couple or individual to talk. Entire presentation lasts about 45 minutes.

Music: Musical arrangements are left to the discretion of the director.

"The Christmas Family" is very inspiring. Yet it is one of the easiest programs that can be presented. It is a blessing to all who participate in it, as well as those who hear and see it.

The Christmas Story

by Nancy L. Funk

The following is a play illustrating the story of Christmas with puppets, scenes from the Bible, and Christmas carols. It is for an audience of all ages, and it can be staged in the church's sanctuary.

Characters: Puppets—Fir Tree
Snow Man
Adam Rabbit
Able Donkey
Actors—Mary
Elisabeth
Joseph
Angel
First Shepherd
Second Shepherd
Third Shepherd
First Wise-man
Second Wise-man
Third Wise-man
Singers—The Children's Choir

Scene 1

(A forest, bathed in moonlight. Fir Tree and Snow Man [hand puppets] are standing as the play begins. The puppeteers are concealed behind risers which are draped with white cloth and placed in front of the church on a painted flat.)

Fir Tree: What a beautiful Christmas eve. There's a full moon falling over the snow. The air is so crisp. Just right for me.

Snow Man: Yes, so crisp. Just right for me.

FT: I wonder when Able Donkey will be here to decorate me. He always comes every Christmas eve.

SM: Yes, every Christmas eve.

FT: He'll put colorful balls and strings of popcorn over my limbs, and I'll be so beautiful when I welcome the Christ child.

SM: Yes, so beautiful when I welcome the Christ child.

FT: Why is it that you repeat everything I say?

SM: You repeat everything I say.

(FT hits SM with a limb.)

FT: See what I mean.

SM: See . . .

(FT puts his limb across SM's mouth.)

FT: Shhh. What do I hear?

(Sound effects of thumping. Growing louder.)

FT: Could it be that silly rabbit again!
He comes here every Christmas eve to bother me.

Adam Rabbit: Hey, fellows, how are you?

FT: Ignore him, and maybe he'll go away.

AR: Well, ready to celebrate Christmas?

FT (punching SM): Shhh. Pretend he's not here.

AR: Down at the bunny hutch, we're all ready with gifts of carrots and cabbage and . . .

FT: Oh, go away. Everyone knows your time is spring and summer, not Christmas. Who ever heard of a rabbit celebrating Christmas?

AR: Why, all my ancestors celebrated Christmas.

(Enter Able Donkey, slowly.)

FT: Oh, there were no rabbits at the stable where Christ was born. Ask Able Donkey. He was there.

Able Donkey (stuttering): Hhhi, ggguys. Nnnice night for Christmas, dddon't you say?

FT: Able Donkey, you tell Adam Rabbit that rabbits weren't around when Christ was born.

50

AD (scratching his head): Wwwell, nnnow lllet's sssee. Ttthere was a sheep, a cccow, a dddonkey—hey that's me! Bbbut a rrrabbit? Hum. (He thinks as he sits.)

AR: Of course, we were there. Why, we've been around since the time AB.

FT: AB! What's AB? There's either the time BC, before Christ, or there's AD, after divinity, or after Christ's birth. But AB! You're way off base!

AR: No, I'm not. According to my great, great, great, great, great grandpappy, AB means—after the bunny!

FT: Oh, why do we have to put up with him? Able Donkey send him away from bothering us.

SM: From bothering us.

FT: And you be quiet!

AD: Nnnow, Fir Tree. III don't think that's very nice. Cccan't Adam Rrrabbit help us celebrate Christmas?

FT: No! His time is later. Let him come out then. He's supposed to give this time to us.

(Ad libs of arguing among the characters.)

Angel (suddenly appearing, startles all the characters): Now, now. Christmas is a time for all to celebrate Christ's birth. He wants you to all love one another.

FT: Me, love a rabbit! What has he done for me?

SM: For me?

AD: Aaand for mmme?

FT: He's tried to nibble my needles and ruin my beauty.

Angel: Fir Tree, Able Donkey, Snow Man! I'm ashamed of you all. Don't you know the true story behind your celebration of Christ's birth?

AD: Sssure, III was there.

Angel: Able, then perhaps you should tell us the story so we can remember the true meaning of Christmas.

(Organ chords allow puppeteers to exit. Extinguishing lights on the riser and lighting the pulpit light will help to divert the audience's attention.)

Scene 2

(A room in a Bible-times home.)

51

Mary (humming as she walks across the room): Oh, you startled me. I . . . (pauses in disbelief.)

Angel (standing in the pulpit and raising arms): Thou that art highly favored, the Lord is with thee: blessed art thou among women. (The Angel's speeches are directly from the King James Version.)

Mary: I don't understand.

Angel: Fear not, Mary: for thou hast found favor with God. Thou shalt conceive in thy womb, and bring forth a son, and shalt call his name Jesus. He shall be great, and shall be called the Son of the Highest; and the Lord God shall give unto him the throne of his father David: and he shall reign over the house of Jacob for ever; and of his kingdom there shall be no end.

Mary: How shall this be, seeing I know not a man?

Angel: The Holy Ghost shall come upon thee, and the power of the Highest shall overshadow thee: therefore also that holy thing which shall be born of thee shall be called the Son of God.

(Dim lights and then turn them back on to give the effect of another time. Enter Elisabeth.)

Elisabeth (calling to Mary): Mary, cousin, how are you today?

Mary (turns to look at Elisabeth): Elisabeth, cousin, I am fine. I was just thinking about what the angel said.

Elisabeth: Whom, Mary? There's no one else here.

Mary: The angel that appeared to me before I came to visit you.

Elisabeth: Angel?

Mary: Yes, an angel. He said I would conceive a male child without a husband. It would be a divine act of God, for the child would be the Son of God.

Elisabeth: Mary, you, indeed, are blessed among women. The babe leaped in my womb. I, too, carry a child given to me by the Lord after many years of barrenness. An angel appeared to my husband and told him I should bear a son whose name would be John.

Mary (hugging Elisabeth): My soul doth magnify the Lord, and my spirit rejoices in God my Savior. He has done mighty things in showing His mercy upon generation after generation. He has scattered the proud, put down the mighty, and filled the hungry. He has remembered Israel as He promised to our father Abraham.

(Pull curtains.)

Congregation (sings): "What Child Is This?"

Scene 3

(Moonlight and stars shine on Mary and Joseph as they travel to Bethlehem.)

Mary: Husband, I fear I cannot travel any longer.

Joseph: Come, Mary. I know you have suffered greatly from the many days on the road. But did not a decree come from Caesar Augustus that all the world should be taxed?

Mary: I know, Joseph. It is the law that we return to our native city for taxation. But the child is heavy. I think my time has come.

Joseph: Good wife, why don't you get back on the donkey as I have suggested?

Mary: No, Joseph, for he is old and already ladened with our belongings. To ride him more would be too much for him. We are going so slowly now because he needs to rest often.

Joseph (crosses to the other side of Mary and looks into the distance and laughs): Yes, he's stopped several yards behind us to nibble the grass. The law has no urgency for him. But the child? Are you certain that the time has come? We have no one here to help us; no family.

Mary (laughing): Do not be afraid, Joseph. I know that God will be with us, for we are obeying Him.

Joseph: But perhaps we should try to reach Bethlehem. There we can find an inn where you will be comfortable. And possibly a midwife can help you.

Mary: Yes, that would be nice.

Joseph (running to the next hill or aisle and looking): Over the hill is Bethlehem. If we can make it there . . .

Mary: Coming, Joseph. We must find a place to stay.

(They walk a few steps and she stops, pondering a question.)

Mary: Joseph, I have never mentioned this to you, but it has entered my thoughts at many times. When we were married, I already was with child. Are you ashamed of me?

Joseph (after a moment's thought): At first I was not willing to go into the public places with you, for I knew it was not my child. But *not* after an angel of the Lord appeared, saying, "Fear not to take unto thee Mary thy wife: for that which is conceived in her is of the Holy Ghost. And she shall bring forth a son, and thou shalt call his name Jesus: for he shall save his people from their sins."

Mary (runs to Joseph and hugs him): It is good, Joseph. You are a good man. And we are fulfilling the prophecy: "Behold, a virgin shall be with child, and shall bring forth a son, and they shall call his name Immanuel, which being interpreted is, God with us."

Joseph: Come, let us go. For it is God's will.

(Pull curtains.)

Scene 4

(Field for sheep—a painted flat and bales of straw. Two shepherds are talking and laughing.)

1st Shepherd (a young boy): What a beautiful night. Ah, moon, show us thy beauty.

2nd Shepherd: Come on, stop gawking at the moon and have something to eat. What's the time?

3rd Shepherd: (looking at the sky): About midnight, I'd say.

2nd Shepherd: We've a long night ahead of us.

3rd Shepherd: What a bore! Spending my life watching these dumb animals.

1st Shepherd: You shouldn't look upon your job like that. Why, if we don't watch them, they will become lost or attacked by wild animals.

3rd Shepherd: Ah, but we could be having fun in the village.

2nd Shepherd: Instead, here we sit with cold food and sheep for company.

3rd Shepherd: And don't forget to mention a dumb

shepherd who talks to the moon (laughs).

1st Shepherd: Hey, look over there . . . toward Bethlehem. In the sky! What is it?

2nd Shepherd: Aw, nothing. You're seeing the moon at "thy beauty."

(The other two shepherds laugh and continue to eat.)

1st Shepherd: Seriously, there seems to be something in the heavens.

(Children's choir in the background softly sings one verse of "Away in a Manger.")

1st Shepherd (continues after the singing has stopped and the children are humming): And I hear singing. Glorious singing, beautiful singing.

3rd Shepherd: How does he do it? Already he's imagining things.

2nd Shepherd: Hey, I'm getting sleepy. I can't hold my eyes open.

3rd Shepherd: I am, too.

1st Shepherd: Shepherds, look! This is unbelievable! It's like the sky has opened and is filling with angels.

3rd Shepherd: Angels, phooey . . . (falls asleep.)

2nd Shepherd: Angels? **He's crazy** . . . (falls asleep).

(The humming in the background gets louder. The 1st Shepherd goes to the other shepherds and shakes them, trying to wake them.)

1st Shepherd: Please wake up and see this spectacle.

(Light falls behind the shepherds to reveal the Angel.)

Angel: Fear not: for, behold, I bring you good tidings of great joy, which shall be to all people.

(The two shepherds awaken and they all huddle in fear.)

2nd Shepherd: What's happening?

3rd Shepherd: Who are you?

1st Shepherd: Speak more!

Angel: "For unto you is born this day in the city of David a Saviour, which is Christ the Lord. And this shall be a sign unto you; Ye shall find the babe wrapped in swaddling clothes, lying in a manger."

(Children's choir enters to stand around the shepherds and sing the second verse of "Away in a Manger.")

Angel (continuing at the end of the verse, while the children are humming): "Glory to God in the highest, and on

earth peace, good will toward men.''
(Angel and choir exit singing or humming.)

1st Shepherd (speaking after the Angel and choir have exited): Let us now go unto Bethlehem.

2nd Shepherd: We'll see this thing which has come to pass.

3rd Shepherd: Which the Lord has made known unto us.

Shepherds (together): Praise be to God!

(Pull curtains.)

Congregation: ''It Came Upon the Midnight Clear'' or ''Hark! the Herald Angels Sing''

Scene 5

(Three Wise-men sing ''We Three Kings of Orient'' at the back of the church as the field scene changes to scene with Mary, Joseph, and the babe. As they come slowly down the aisles, the Wise-men say the following words across the heads of the audience.)

1st Wise-man: Where is He that is born the King of the Jews?

2nd Wise-man: We have seen His star in the East.

3rd Wise-man: And we are come to worship Him.

1st Wise-man: We have been sent by King Herod to find the young child.

3rd Wise-man: We bring Him gifts of gold, frankincense, and myrrh.

2nd Wise-man: Herod told us when we find the child to return so that he might come and worship Him, too.

1st Wise-man: But did not an angel of the Lord appear in a dream telling us not to return to Herod?

3rd Wise-man: Yes, so when we have worshiped the child, let us depart to our own country by another way.

2nd Wise-man: Behold, the star!

1st Wise-man: It is as the prophets have said. Our Savior and Redeemer has come.

Scene 6

(The Wise-men kneel while Mary and Joseph silently look

on. The congregation sings "Silent Night, Holy Night."
After the last verse, up pops Able Donkey and Adam Rabbit from behind a bale of straw. This staging may seem to be a tight squeeze for all characters, but it can be done.)

AD: Wwwell, Aaadam, that's the end of my ssstory of Christmas.

AR: Yeah, I was there. I gave Mary my fur to cover the Christ child.

AD: And I saw the cccloths used to wwwrap Him in. (Thinks for a moment.) Bbbut your fur? Hhhow did you mmmanage to give your fffur to the babe?

AR; Ever wonder why rabbits have short tails?

AD: Oh, Adam, you're ssstretching the tttruth.

AR: No, Able, only my tale!

AD: Oh, I see. You're pulling another one of your jokes on us.

(All characters pop up on the hay and everyone sings "Joy to the World." During the last verse all actors exit, leaving the babe to be bathed in a blue light. The congregation joyfully exits to an organ refrain.)

Mary's Little Baby

by Carolyn Scheidies

Parts: Six speakers, Mary, Joseph, shepherds, angels, children.

Props: Appropriate costumes, manger, doll, spotlight. (Center stage: Manger scene with Mary and Joseph. Speakers form a semicircle in the background.)

Speaker #1: (Spotlight center stage.)
Mary's little baby,
A son for Joseph's care,
And yet this little bundle
Was a very special heir.

Speaker #2: (Speakers raise hands.)
The Son, God's Son,
Came to earth that night,
When angels sang a chorus
And the star shone bright.

(Spotlight stage left. Show angel chorus before frightened shepherds.)

Speaker #3: Angels sang their chorus

To shepherds in the field,
And when they heard the message,
Bells of joy pealed. (Bells sound off stage.)

(Angels leave. Shepherds go to the manger and kneel. Spotlight follows.)

Speaker #4: The shepherds left their sheep
Under the dark night sky,
They went to worship Jesus,
Without a question why.

(Children join shepherds.)

Speaker #5: We, too, can come to Jesus,
As the shepherds long ago.
For Jesus, the heir of Heaven,
Came to make it so.

(Speaker #6 comes to front of stage before the manger scene. As he speaks he reaches out his arms to the audience. Then he, too, kneels before the manger.)

Speaker #6: So at this Christmas season
Kneel down and worship Him.
Ask the One who loves you
To come and dwell within.

I Love My Lord Jesus

by Evelyn Stenbock

(An exercise for seven Juniors. Each child repeats two lines. They shout the third line in unison.

I love my Lord Jesus;
 I know why He came—
TO FREE US FROM THE DEVIL!

I love my Lord Jesus,
 I know who He is—
THE SON OF GOD!

I love my Lord Jesus,
 I know what He did—
DIED FOR OUR SINS!

I love my Lord Jesus,
 I know how He won—
ROSE FROM THE DEAD!

I love my Lord Jesus,
 I know what to do—
OBEY AND FOLLOW HIM!

I love my Lord Jesus,
 I know where He is—
IN HEAVEN, GETTING READY FOR US!

I love my Lord Jesus,
 I know when He'll come back—
ANYTIME!

Your Choice

by Evelyn Stenbock

An exercise for six Juniors. Make placards for each of the first lines, which the child will hold up (or place on a flannelboard) as he speaks.

MY INN WAS FULL!
I looked upon the tired folks
   With anger and with scorn.
How could I know that very night
   The Savior would be born?

I WAS JEALOUS!
The message that a king was born
   Was shattering to me.
I couldn't know the royal child
   Would hang upon a tree!

GO AWAY—NOT TONIGHT!
I don't have time for Jesus now;
   No room to let Him stay,
For I've a million things to do.
   Tell Him to go away!

KEEP OUT OF MY LIFE!
Now wait a minute! Submit to whom?
   Forget it. I'm my boss.

I don't believe a word you say.
    Don't talk about *my* loss.

WHAT WILL YOU DO WITH JESUS?
The choice is yours—God offers you
    Salvation, hope, and peace,
Security, eternal life,
    And joys that never cease.

DON'T SAY NO!
It's up to you. Imagine that
    He's knocking at your door.
Eternity's a long, long time—
    Wrong choices have been made before!

EVERY KNEE SHALL BOW *(unison)*
At the name of Jesus every knee shall bow . . . and
every tongue shall confess that Jesus Christ is Lord, to
the glory of God, the Father.

Five Children

by Velda Blumhagen

Five children stood outside
An open church door.
One went in and sang a song,
Then there were four.
(First child steps back.)

Four children near the church
Wondered what they'd see.
Another went inside the church,
Then there were three.
(Second child steps back.)

Three lonely children
Had nothing else to do.
Another went inside the church,
Then there were two.
(Third child steps back.)

Two children left alone
Longed to join the fun.
Another went inside the church,
Then there was one.
(Fourth child steps back.)

This child also went inside
To sing the Christmas song.
All the children had a part,
In church where they belong.
(Fifth child steps back with others.)

All five children sing: "Away in a Manger." (Or another song of choice.)